Echoes of the Soul

Echoes of the Soul

Christian Poetry

Book One of the Heart and Soul Christian Poetry Collection

Esselle Davis

Echoes of the Soul
Christian Poetry
Book One of the Heart and Soul Christian Poetry Collection
First Edition
ISBN: 9798685765437
© 2020 Esselle Davis
All rights reserved

DEDICATION

Echoes of the Soul
Christian Poetry
is dedicated to:

My husband Tony
My daughter Mandy
The memory of my Mama, Mary
The memory of my Daddy, Doyle

PREFACE

My journey to writing poetry began when I wanted to send an online greeting to a friend of mine. I couldn't find anything that I liked, or anything that had the message I wanted to send to her. I had a thought to write my own and I thought about what I wanted to say. I wanted it to be something about an angel, so I looked at many images of angels and I finally found one. Looking at that particular picture gave me the thoughts that eventually became a poem. I had managed to write one poem and tried my hand at writing a few more. After receiving encouragement from family and friends I continued to write. There have been times I moved away from writing, but I always come back to it. I find peace in writing and enjoy my time spent writing.

14 And as Moses lifted up the serpent in the wilderness, even so must the Son of man be lifted up:
15 That whosoever believeth in him should not perish, but have eternal life.
16 For God so loved the world, that he gave his only begotten Son, that whosoever believeth in him should not perish, but have everlasting life.
17 For God sent not his Son into the world to condemn the world; but that the world through him might be saved.

John 3:16 King James Version

Contents

THANK YOU LORD

Thank you Lord
For all you do
You lift me up
When I'm feeling blue

You gave your life
To set me free
When I called out to You
You answered my plea

Your precious blood
Washed away my sin
You gave me hope
And peace within

Dear Jesus you are
A friend so true
Thank you again
For all you do

AT THE FEET OF JESUS

When I get to Heaven
There will be many sights to see
But at the feet of Jesus
Is where I long to be

When I get there
The joy will before me unfold
But at the feet of Jesus
I will behold

The one who died
To set me free
And gave this gift
To a sinner like me

At the feet of Jesus
Is where I long to be
Giving praise to the One
Who died for me

JUDGMENT DAY

When you stand before God will He say
My child welcome home
Or will He say depart from me
Ye I've not known

If you are saved in Heaven
You will find joy and peace
If you are not saved in Hell
Your torment will never cease

So my friends
In your salvation be sure
Because saved or not
Your soul will forever endure

Accept Jesus and the love
He does convey
Heaven will be your reward
Come judgment day

WHEN DEATH HAS TAKEN AWAY

When death has taken away
Someone we hold dear
Our hearts are filled with sadness
It is difficult to find cheer

The loss we feel
We can't comprehend
We just want the heartbreak
To come to an end

By our sadness
We may feel confined
But if we hold on
Comfort we can find

Jesus will comfort us
With His tender loving care
And we find peace knowing
Our loved one is in Heaven so fair

ONLY JESUS

Only Jesus
Can satisfy your soul
He will cleanse your sins
And make you whole

Trust in Him
And you will see
Only Jesus
Can set you free

Only Jesus
Gives the gift, of eternal life
Believe in Him
He will relieve you, of your strife

If you want to go
To Heaven so fair
Only Jesus
Can take you there

IN ALL HIS GLORY

Jesus was a king
But He wasn't treated as one
Even though He was indeed
God's only Son

He came here because
He loved mankind so much
But instead He was mocked
Tormented and such

One day in Heaven
Jesus will be crowned king
Knowing I will be there
Makes my heart sing

I hope you are saved
And will also be there to see
Jesus the King
In all His glory

IT IS YOUR CHOICE

My friends we will
All live eternally
Either in happiness
Or pure misery

If you've accepted Jesus as your Savior
And been saved by God's grace
You will live forever in Heaven
A most beautiful place

But if you have pushed
Jesus away
Your eternity will be spent in torment
Forever in Hell you will stay

So my friends when your life is over
In Heaven you can rejoice
Or suffer an eternity of torment in Hell
It is your choice

GOD'S PAINTING

As dawn gently breaks
Color paints the sky
The sun breaks the horizon
Beauty fills my eye

All day long
God's creation I see
A wonderful gift
He bestows to me

As dusk falls o'er the land
Heavenward I gaze
The sun sinks low
The sky is ablaze

Each and every day
A masterpiece I view
The beauty which surrounds me
It is a work of art so true

A glorious painting for me
From the Father above
Created by His hand
Colored with His love

PREPARE A PLACE

The sins of the world upon Him
The penalty had been applied
Jesus bore my sin and shame
On a cross He hanged and died

In a borrowed tomb they placed Him
A stone was rolled at the door
Many thought they were free of Him
And He would live no more

One morning a surprise did wait
The stone was rolled away
Jesus had risen from the dead
He escaped death's sway

Jesus returned to His Father
To Heaven He arose
He went to prepare a place
For the believer's eternal repose

THE TRIBULATION

One day Jesus
Will return in the sky
To take God's children to their new home
In Heaven on high

When they get there
Happiness and peace they will find
But it won't be that way
For those left behind

As Jesus opens
The seven seals
The earth will be inflicted
With many ills

As the angels the
Seven trumpets sound
Fire and brimstone
Will rain to the ground

As Jesus pours the
Seven vials of wrath
Torment and misery
Will fill their path

The sun moon and stars
Will darken by one third
Many will wish they had listened
To God's Holy Word

The seas and rivers
Will turn to blood
Horrors will fall on earth
In an unrelenting flood

The earth will be tormented
With horrors that you cannot envision
Do not be left here
Because of indecision

Jesus offers you a way
These horrors to elude
Accept Him as Savior
And your soul will be renewed

Once you accept salvation
You will be one of Christ's own
The terrors of the Tribulation
To you will be unknown

THE STONE WAS ROLLED AWAY

The body of Jesus was taken from the cross
And placed in a borrowed tomb
Many did not know it
But Heaven's Rose again would bloom

His body now was lifeless
A linen cloth it wore
Silent in death He laid there
A stone was rolled at the door

Jesus had told His disciples
From death He would arise
He knew death on the cross
Would not be His demise

The chains of death were broken
Jesus woke from His repose
Death could not bind Him
From death He arose

The women came to visit
As a new day did dawn
They found the tomb empty
The Savior, He was gone

The tomb could not hold Him

In death He would not stay

Jesus Christ is risen

The stone was rolled away

PLEA FOR DEATH

Hearts were broken watching you suffer
Hearts were broken letting you go
You have gone to live with Jesus
His love you did know

You are no longer with us
But a mansion is your new home
You are surrounded by treasures
That here are unknown

While here on earth, in pain
In your bed, you would lie
Wondering why God
Would not let you die

Through your pain and suffering
You often despaired
But you had to wait until
Your mansion was prepared

Once the finishing touches
Were in place
The death angel came and took you
To the Lord's embrace

Your earthly suffering
Was not in vain
For you are now walking with Jesus
Along Heaven's golden lane

You are now living in Heaven
Happy and free
For the Lord heard and answered
Your humble plea

A TEMPORARY GOODBYE

Don't weep for me
I am at peace
From my pain
Death gave me release

As I left this life
I crossed through death's door
My feet gently landed
On Heaven's golden shore

I got to see my Savior
Who died to set me free
Loved ones gone on before
I am now able to see

For family and friends
Whom I left behind
Please remember this
When I come to your mind

My body is now
Just an empty shell
My soul is with Jesus
And there it does dwell

I'll be waiting and when
Your time does come
I'll be there to greet you
When your race has been run

When you think of me
Please don't cry
Because death is just
A temporary goodbye

HELL

No matter what
Some may say
Hell is real
And growing each day

It is a place for those
Who have not accepted the Lord
Their eternity is torment
And misery with no reward

In Hell the worm
Does not die
There will be no one
To hear you cry

There will no mercy
For you to obtain
Forever in this misery
You will ever remain

No matter how much you beg
Or how much you plead
This terrible torment
Will never recede

Horrors untold

Will around you impend

This torture for you

Will never end

So my friend if you don't accept Salvation

A gift from Jesus so true

An eternity in hell is waiting

Waiting for you

VICTORY I HAVE WON

Even though I am saved
By God's marvelous grace
There are still times
When hardship I face

Satan would have me believe
That Jesus had forsaken me
But when I pray to my Savior
He will hear my plea

He will comfort me
And carry me through
He is a friend
A friend so true

Even in trials
I will offer Him praise
He will be with me
Till the end of my days

Then I will go to Heaven
To see my new home
To live with Jesus
Nevermore to roam

There may be times
When things go awry
And happiness in my life
May be in short supply

But since I accepted Jesus
God's precious holy Son
I may lose a battle
But the victory I have won

WHEN I CALLED ON YOUR NAME

Lord there are times when
By troubles I am bound
I want to call out to You
But it seems You're not around

I feel that I have to face
These trials on my own
It seems You have left me
Lonely and alone

Then Lord I begin to wonder
What this feeling of desertion is about
Then I realize it is Satan
Trying to make me doubt

Satan tries his best
To fill me with fear
He does not want me
To feel You near

Then Lord I remember
That You are my dearest friend
I remember You will be with me
Until the very end

I enter into prayer
And call out to Thee
I feel Your love
And Satan has to flee

Your love and blessings
I now can claim
For You heard me
When I called on Your name

I DID NOT DENY

I am glad the
Savior's love I did not deny
For one day I will bid
This world goodbye

He is the Son
Of God above
He loves me with
An endless love

He is with me through
Good, bad, calm and fear
He saved my soul
And gave me cheer

I can feel His love
When to Him I pray
He is there to guide me
Each and every day

He will be with me
Till I take my last breath
He will be there
When my eyes close in death

As my time comes
And I cross death's sea
Jesus will be there
Waiting for me

He will then take me
To my new home, in Heaven on high
Because His gift of eternal life
I did not deny

WHEN THE EVENING COMES

As the evening comes
And the sun starts to set
I look over my day
And the people I've met

In my mind I review
The things I've said and done
Did I share your love Lord
With anyone

Did I tell them
You gave your life
To save their soul
And relieve their strife

As the evening comes
I get ready to rest
I thank you Lord
For I am blessed

You were there with me
All through my day
Leading and guiding me
As I went along my way

Dear Jesus thank you

For all that You've done

Thank you for being there

As today's race was run

And as the sound of the night

Sweetly hums

I rest in your love Lord

When the evening comes

ARC OF PROMISE

When I see a rainbow
Spanning the sky
I think of God and His love
Which comes in great supply

After the flood God placed a rainbow
For Noah to view
As a symbol of a promise
That would always remain true

I had a promise
Made unto me
When Jesus saved my soul
And from my sins set me free

Jesus promised me
Eternal life
I will live it in Heaven
Free from suffering and strife

I carry this promise
With me day to day
For Jesus is with me
As I go along my way

The blood of Jesus
Has covered my heart
Like a protective arc
That will never depart

The rainbow is an arc of promise
Against a worldwide flood
I escaped Hell through my arc of promise
Which is Jesus my Savior's blood

WHERE WILL YOU SPEND ETERNITY

My dear friends
I know this for sure
That each of our souls
Will forever endure

It is up to God to say
When you bid this world adieu
But my friend where you spend eternity
Is entirely up to you

You can chose eternal life
In Heaven filled with everlasting peace
You can chose eternal damnation
In Hell where your torment will never cease

If you accept the gift of Salvation
That Jesus so freely gave
When you let Him in your heart
Jesus your soul will save

Then you will be saved
By God's wonderful grace
One day for you Heaven will be
A new resting place

You will stand before God
With Jesus, a friend divine
He will reply "Father
This one is mine"

You will enter in
To glorious Heaven above
You will surrounded by beauty
And God's pure love

You will live in mansion
And walk on a street of gold
Beauty never seen on earth
You will now behold

But if you do not accept
The gift of eternal life
Hell will be waiting
Full of suffering and strife

You will stand before God
Needing a friend that is true
Jesus will reply "depart from me
I never knew you"

You will be cast into Hell

Tormented by flame
Because the gift of Salvation
You never did claim

You will be in a place
Where the worm does not die
You will beg for mercy
But no one will hear your cry

You will hope and wish
For an end to come
But to this torment
You will never succumb

So my friend you see
We all have a choice
With Salvation through Jesus
In Heaven we will forever rejoice

But if you choose
This wonderful gift to ignore
You will spend eternity in Hell
Tormented forever more

IN THE VALLEY

I was in a valley
My spirit was low
I was miserable
And filled with woe

I did not understand
The hardships I did face
Why oh why was
I in this place

So I asked God
Why oh why must things be this way
Do you find pleasure
When I'm filled with dismay?

I then asked God
Why do you torture me?
He answered my child
Why can you not see

When you were happy and well
Every sweet day
You took for granted the blessings
I sent your way

You went along
Without a care
You did not talk to Me
Ever in Prayer

Even as
Your happiness grew
I did not get
Even a simple thank you

But when hardships
You go through
You come to Me
Your spirit to renew

God said my child
I love you so
That's why I'm there for you
When you're feeling low

To lift you up
And restore your delight
To help you through
And brighten your sight

God said when you are in the valley

That's when you want Me near
I give you strength
To help you persevere

But when you are on the mountain
And can see far and wide
During those happy times
You pushed me aside

God then said my child I do not desire
To see you filled with sorrow
I want you to have hope
For a bright new tomorrow

God said I want you to be
On the mountain high
With the happiness in your heart
In great supply

But there are times when
A valley you must go through
To remember that
I am there for You

He said my child
I hope you understand

It's when you're in the valley

That you cling to My hand

FROM THE ASHES OF WINTER COMES THE BEAUTY OF SPRING

From the ashes of winter
Comes the beauty of spring
After the cold
Warmth, sunshine does bring

Winters crumpled leaves are like ashes
Lying on the ground
Eventually new plant life appears
And springs greenery abounds

Life also changes
Just as the seasons do
Cycles of life
Mama and Daddy went through

They each had a long life
Full of moments good and bad
Sometimes they were happy
Sometimes they were sad

At different times in their life
They each accepted Christ's loving call
At death they would see Heaven

Because Jesus gave His all

As they accepted the gift of salvation
Their hearts joyfully soared
Knowing an eternity in Heaven
Would one day, be their reward

For Mama sickness was like winter
Cold and dark
But she knew on a joyful journey
She soon would embark

For Daddy sickness was like winter
Dark and cold
But he knew Heavenly wonders
He soon would behold

Much pain and suffering
They each endured
But by the blood of Jesus
Their souls were insured

As their lives each drew closer
And closer to an end
We all knew soon, life's last breath
They would expend

When to a life of sickness
They could no longer cling
I imagine they heard the flutter
Of sweet angel wings

They each knew death to them s
Sickness would bring
But they did not fear the pain
Of death's lonely cold sting

For they each were saved
By God's wonderful grace
They would meet death
Wrapped in God's loving embrace

As the death angel
Took them, each gently away
They entered the land
Of bright eternal day

As they entered eternal happiness
Their souls began to sing
They were now in the presence
Of Jesus the Heavenly King

Their cycle of life

Was now complete
They were now a part
Of Heaven's elite

Death had taken them
To beautiful Heaven above
They would be forever ensconced
In God's pure love

Meeting Jesus in Heaven
Their hearts leapt
Angels led the way
As they each stepped

Through the scattered ashes of winter
That sickness did bring
Into the majestic beauty
Of Heaven's glorious eternal spring

YOU WERE NOT THERE

Last night I dreamed I went to Heaven
It was such a beautiful sight
But I could not find you anywhere
Though I tried with all my might

I saw the saints and angels
Gathered round God's eternal throne
It was the most wonderful view
My eyes had ever known

I approached the crowd
And asked them all
But of seeing you there
They could not recall

Then I walked about the city
Upon the streets of gold
I felt that surely soon
Your face I would behold

I saw the glorious mansions
In the city where the day will never end
But no matter how hard I searched
I could not find you my precious friend

I thought that I could find you
Resting beside the crystal sea
But you were not there either
And this began to worry me

Then Jesus approached me
And said my child what troubles you so
I replied to Him Lord I can't find my friend
I have searched for them to and fro

As Jesus looked into my face
Tears filled His eyes
He said my child your friend is in Hell
Can't you hear their cries

I said my Lord how can this be
I saw them every day
We walked and talked together
As we went along our way

Jesus said
My child you shared your petty thoughts
With people everywhere
But about the souls in jeopardy
You didn't seem to care

You never shared with them
The basis of your belief
You never even asked them
If their souls had found relief

I said my Lord I loved them so
I did not want to offend
Jesus said but they are now in Hell
Their torment will never end

I cried dear Lord please send me back
And give me one more chance
I now know that when it comes to You
I have to take a stance

I have to share your precious love
With everyone I see
And tell them how you gave your life
On the cross of Calvary

As I awoke and sat up in bed
The tears down my face did stream
It was then that I realized
It had only been a dream

So now my friend when we meet again

I will ask you how you feel
I will also share with you a story
That Heaven and Hell are very real

I will ask have you let Jesus
Come into your heart
I will tell you if you haven't
When we die we will forever be apart

I will ask you to accept Jesus
Here this very day
Because you never know
When death will come your way

My dear friend I beg of you
Please accept the gift that Jesus gave
He is waiting for you to ask
He then your soul will save

Jesus will then give you peace
That Satan can't destroy
Then when death comes to visit you
Heaven you will enjoy

HOW MUCH DO YOU LOVE ME

During a time when
I was feeling blue
I began to question
If Christ's love for me was true

I wrestled with these thoughts
No peace of mind I found
It got to the point
Where by my question I was bound

I prayed to God the Father
To let me see
Just how much
The Savior loved me

The answer came to me
In a dream that night
What I was to discover
Would relieve my plight

My dream did take me
To a time long gone
Into my dream
I was soon drawn

I was walking with
Jesus so dear
I could reach out and touch Him
He was so near

I asked Him, Lord
How much do you love me?
He answered my child
Do you not see?

That what the Father
Sent me to do
Is for everyone
Including you

That answer did not satisfy me
I was filled with unrest
I am sure to the others there
I was becoming a pest

My dream went on
And continued until
I was staring at a cross
Calvary's hill

Jesus was hung

On that cross there
There were many in the crowd
That didn't seem to care

Crucify Him, Crucify Him
They did chant
Soon the majority
Took part in the rant

But Jesus with compassion
Said ever so true
Father forgive them
For they know not what they do

The end of Christ's torture
Was drawing near
I wanted my answer
And I wanted here

I said, Jesus will you please
Answer my plea
Lord, oh Lord
How much do you love me?

It is finished
The Savior cried

The spirit left Him
And then He died

While on the cross
Jesus suffered and bled
I realized for all
His blood He had shed

The answer then
Became crystal clear
Christ's love for all
Is very sincere

Jesus was sent by
The Father above
He gave His life
Out of a pure sweet love

Then it was as if
Jesus spoke to my heart
A question to me
He did impart

He said, I died on the cross
To set you free

Now my child the question is

How much do you love me?

FROM THE MANGER TO THE CROSS

Jesus is the Son
Of God the Father above
He was sent to earth
On a mission of love

Jesus started His earthly life
In a stable so bare
To the shepherds in the field
News of His birth the angels did declare

Mary and Joseph did not have
For this precious baby a bed
So they laid Him in a manger
Where the animals were fed

Even as a child Jesus knew
The path He must walk
He was in the temple
And with the doctors He did talk

When Joseph and Mary found Him in the temple
She said my child why did you trouble us so

He replied

"I must be about my Father's business"
This you must know

Jesus was baptized by John
In the river one day
Those that were there
Heard God's voice say

"This is my beloved Son
In whom I am well pleased"
Jesus was sent here so that
Troubled souls could be eased

Satan tempted Jesus
In the wilderness forty days
But Jesus was never fooled
By Satan's wicked ways

Jesus healed the deaf
The blind and the lame
All to give glory to
God's Holy name

All about the land
God's goodness He spread
Jesus had the power

To raise the dead

There were those who did not like Jesus
They felt He was a threat
They did not realize He was
The only one who could pay sins debt

Their hatred for Jesus
Was growing rife
They decided that they wanted
To end His life

Jesus was placed on trial
Though He had done nothing wrong
The earthly mission of Jesus
Was moving along

His trial came to an end
Jesus was sentenced to die
Because the will of God the Father
He would not defy

Jesus was hanged on a cross
On Calvary's hill
He was fulfilling
His Father's will

As Jesus hanged there
He was tormented and mocked
By the treatment He received
Those who loved Him were shocked

Jesus cried

"Father forgive them
For they know not what they do"
I imagine He thought they do not realize
My blood is the path that will lead them to You

As He hanged on the cross
His body filled with suffering and pain
I imagine He thought if just one accepts me
My death was not in vain

Jesus walked the path
From the manger to the cross
To be a source of salvation
For the souls that were lost

He was born in a stable
Humble and meek
He died on a cross
His body beaten and weak

Jesus could have called angels

To lift this burden from Him

But for the people with no hope

Jesus knew that He must do this for them

HE'S WAITING RIGHT THERE

I had hardened my heart
And pushed Jesus away
I thought I was fine
But I was going astray

Then one night I had a dream
That at first, seemed strange
I did not realize it, but
It was time for a change

I saw a man
Staring at me
It made me curious
I had to go see

What exactly
He was doing here
I needed no one
I had made that clear

It made me angry
That he had invaded my dream
But I would soon see things
Are not always what they seem

As I approached him
The light glistened on tears in his eyes
The closer I got
I could hear his sad cries

I decided that
I had to know
What was troubling
This poor man so

As I approached him
I began to speak
Pardon me sir
Why are you so bleak

He answered a loved one has left me
They need me no more
They do not realize
Them I still adore

I had promised to be with them
Until the end
I promised I would be
Their most faithful friend

I had walked with them

Through day and through night
After a while with me
They found no delight

I told them one day
They would have a new home
In a land filled with joy
And treasures unknown

The man said to me
I gave them my all
But on me no longer
Did they ever call

There was something
So familiar about this man
I had tried to figure it out
Since the dream began

I decided it was time
For me to depart
Even though this sweet man
Had broken my heart

I said to this man
I'm sorry you are hurting so

But the time has come
For me to go

Sir if you don't mind me asking
Who made you so blue
He looked me in the eyes
And said my child it was you

I replied, I'm sorry sir
But we have never met
He said my child
Do you think I would ever forget

You let me in your heart
Many years ago
When you came to me
You were feeling low

So crystal clear
Things then became
I was talking to Jesus
And I was filled with shame

Jesus said my child
I waited for your return
Even though for me

You had no concern

I said, Jesus I am sorry
I pushed you away
Please walk with me again
This I do pray

Jesus said my child
I hear your plea
I been here waiting
Right where you left me

I am now walking
Again with the Lord
Without fail
My spirit He restored

Now my friend you know
What I have been through
I wanted to share
My story with you

I am sharing this
Out of concern
I hope you benefit
From what I did learn

If you've turned your back on Jesus
And you're filled with despair
Journey back to where you left Him
He's waiting right there

Alphabetical Index of Poems

COLOPHON

Echoes of the Soul Christian Poetry Book One in the Heart and Soul Christian Poetry Collection is independently published..